Unveiling the Wealthy Veil:

Inside the Secrets of Billionaires

By Todd R. Harden

Table Of Content:

Introduction

chapter 1: who is a Billionaire?

- importance of a Billionaire
- characteristics of a Billionaire

chapter 2: 7 crazy facts of a Billionaire
-Impact of a Billionaire on society

chapter 3: Do's and Don't of a Billionaire
-the do's of a Billionaire
- the don't of a Billionaire

chapter 4: The Billionaire mindset
-business ideas that can generate wealth
-list of online investments that can generate wealth

chapter 5: conclusion

Introduction:

Welcome to a world veiled in mystery and fascination—the realm of billionaires. They are the modern-day titans, the epitome of unimaginable wealth and success. We see their luxurious lifestyles, their extravagant mansions, and their high-profile ventures, and we wonder: What does it take to join their illustrious ranks? How do they navigate the complex landscapes of business, finance, and life to amass such staggering fortunes?

In **"Unveiling the Wealthy Veil: Inside the Secrets of Billionaires,"** we embark on a captivating journey of discovery. This book is an invitation to explore the hidden depths beneath the surface-level narratives of billionaire success stories. It goes beyond the glossy magazines and headlines, seeking to unravel the enigmatic qualities and profound insights that have propelled these individuals to the pinnacles of wealth.

As we peel back the layers of secrecy and delve into the inner workings of billionaires' minds, we encounter a world rich with wisdom, innovation, and unparalleled determination. It becomes apparent that their triumphs are not merely a result of luck or chance, but rather a product of meticulous strategies, calculated risks, and relentless pursuit of their visions.

Through extensive research, firsthand accounts, and in-depth interviews, "Unveiling the Wealthy Veil" reveals the principles, philosophies, and habits that have shaped the lives of billionaires. We uncover their unorthodox approaches to wealth creation, their unique perspectives on investing, and the profound impact of their networks and relationships. More than a mere exploration of financial strategies, this book delves into the essence of the billionaire mindset—the audacity to think big, the ability to spot opportunities where others see obstacles, and the unwavering commitment to constant self-improvement.

Moreover, "Unveiling the Wealthy Veil" transcends the realm of money and material abundance. It examines the values that underpin the lives of billionaires—philanthropy, innovation, and the pursuit of purpose. These individuals are not content with amassing wealth for its own sake; they strive to leave a lasting impact on society, leveraging their resources to effect meaningful change.

Whether you're an aspiring entrepreneur, a seasoned investor, or simply curious about the inner workings of extraordinary success, this book is a treasure trove of knowledge, inspiration, and practical wisdom. It challenges conventional thinking, pushes the boundaries of possibility, and empowers you to redefine your relationship with wealth and achievement.

So, prepare to lift the veil and embark on a transformative journey. Join me as we unravel the secrets that lie within the hearts and minds of billionaires. Let **"Unveiling the Wealthy Veil: Inside the Secrets of Billionaires"** be your guide to unlocking the untapped potential within yourself and charting a course towards extraordinary success.

Chapter 1:

Who is a Billionaire?

A person with a net worth of at least $1 billion is considered a billionaire. This often indicates that they have amassed an enormous fortune as a result of their business endeavors, investments, or other revenue streams. Billionaires are frequently viewed as extremely powerful, accomplished people who have the potential to have a big effect on their fields and communities. There is no one description of a billionaire that applies to everybody, although many have qualities in common with one another, including a strong work ethic, a desire for achievement, and a wish to have a beneficial effect on the world.

An ambitious and sometimes unreachable aim for the majority of people is becoming a millionaire. Some people achieve success due to their financial, academic, or opportunistic advantages. Others can take cautious chances, and cultivate their originality, and their capital profitably.

On the other side, some people lose out on the chance to become wealthy because they hurry achievement or don't have a long-term strategy. You can raise your chances of financial accomplishment by utilizing concentration, discipline, and routine frameworks.

- **Importance of a Billionaire:**

Being a billionaire has value beyond only material wealth and social status. Through their investments and generosity, billionaires can have a substantial positive effect on society. They can invest in cutting-edge technology that can enhance people's lives and support philanthropic initiatives and research. Additionally, billionaires frequently boost the economy and create jobs, which may benefit whole nations as well as local communities. Billionaires must be aware of their reputation and the effects their activities have on society since tremendous wealth comes with enormous responsibility. The capacity of billionaires to not only amass fortune but also put it to good use is ultimately what makes them important.

- **Characteristics of a Billionaire:**

Characteristics of a billionaire vary from person to person, as they can come from diverse backgrounds and possess unique qualities. However, there are several common characteristics often associated with billionaires. Here are some of them:

Visionary: Billionaires tend to possess a strong vision and the ability to think big. They can see opportunities and trends that others might overlook and are willing to take risks to pursue their goals.

Persistence and Determination: Building a billion-dollar fortune often requires years of hard work, setbacks, and overcoming obstacles. Billionaires tend to be highly determined individuals who persistently pursue their objectives despite challenges or failures.

Entrepreneurial Mindset: Many billionaires are entrepreneurs who have successfully started and scaled businesses. They possess a mindset that embraces innovation, creativity, and the ability to identify and capitalize on market gaps.

Strong Work Ethic: Billionaires are often known for their exceptional work ethic. They are willing to put in long hours, make sacrifices, and consistently push themselves to achieve their goals.

Passion and Drive: Passion is a common trait among billionaires. They are driven by a genuine enthusiasm for their work and have an unwavering desire to make a significant impact or change in their industry or the world at large.

Resilience: Facing failure and adversity is a part of the journey for many billionaires. They possess resilience, bounce back from setbacks, and learn from their experiences, using failures as opportunities for growth.

Constant Learning and Adaptability: Billionaires have a thirst for knowledge and are lifelong learners. They actively seek new information, stay updated on industry trends, and adapt their strategies accordingly to stay ahead in a rapidly changing world.

Strong Leadership Skills: Many billionaires exhibit exceptional leadership qualities. They can inspire and motivate others, build high-performing teams, delegate effectively, and make decisive decisions when needed.

Financial Acumen: Understanding finance and having a solid grasp of investment strategies is often a characteristic of billionaires. They possess the ability to identify lucrative opportunities, manage risks, and make astute financial decisions.

Philanthropy and Social Impact: Several billionaires are known for their philanthropic endeavors and desire to make a positive difference in society. They use their wealth and influence to support charitable causes and address societal challenges.

It's important to note that while these characteristics can be found in many billionaires, they are not exclusive to them, and individuals can exhibit these qualities without necessarily attaining billionaire status.

Chapter 2

7 crazy facts of a Billionaire

Certainly! Here are seven crazy facts about billionaires:

1. Billionaires can afford some of the most extravagant purchases in the world. For instance, some have purchased private islands, luxurious yachts, or even space travel experiences.

2. The wealth of billionaires can sometimes exceed the GDP of small countries. Their net worth can surpass the economic output of nations, making them incredibly influential and powerful individuals.

3. Some billionaires have unique hobbies and interests. For example, Elon Musk, the CEO of Tesla and SpaceX, has expressed his fascination with space

exploration and has plans to colonize Mars in the future.

4. Billionaires often have access to exclusive and high-end services. They can hire personal chefs, stylists, trainers, and even have their own private security teams.

5. Philanthropy plays a significant role in the lives of many billionaires. They donate substantial amounts of their wealth to charitable causes, foundations, and initiatives that aim to make a positive impact on society.

6. Being a billionaire doesn't necessarily mean a life of leisure. Many billionaires are highly driven individuals who continue to work tirelessly to expand their businesses, invest in new ventures, and create more wealth.

7. Some billionaires have unusual habits or eccentricities. For example, Warren

Buffett, one of the world's most successful investors, is known for his frugal lifestyle despite being incredibly wealthy. He still lives in the same modest house he bought decades ago and prefers to enjoy simple meals at fast-food restaurants.

- **Impact of a Billionaire on society**

The impact of a billionaire on society can be significant and varied. Here are some ways in which billionaires can influence society:

Philanthropy and charitable giving: Many billionaires engage in philanthropic activities and donate a portion of their wealth to various causes. They establish foundations, endowments, and charitable organizations that address issues such as poverty alleviation, education, healthcare, environmental conservation, and scientific research. Their contributions can make a substantial positive impact by funding projects and initiatives that benefit society as a whole.

Job creation and economic growth: Billionaires often play a crucial role in driving economic growth. Through their entrepreneurial ventures and business investments, they create job opportunities for a large number of people. Their companies generate employment, promote innovation, and contribute to the overall prosperity of communities and economies.

Innovation and technological advancements: Many billionaires are pioneers in their respective fields and have revolutionized industries through innovation and technological advancements. Their investments in research and development, startups, and cutting-edge technologies often lead to breakthroughs that transform entire sectors, improve quality of life, and create new possibilities for societal progress.

Influence on public policy: Due to their wealth and influence, billionaires can have significant sway over public policy and political discourse. They may engage in advocacy, lobbying, and campaign contributions to shape policies that align with their interests or philanthropic goals. This influence can impact areas such as taxation, regulation, social issues, and public initiatives.

Wealth inequality and social issues: The concentration of wealth among billionaires has been a subject of debate and concern. Critics argue that extreme wealth disparities can perpetuate social inequalities and create an imbalance of power. Discussions around fair taxation, income redistribution, and social justice often involve considerations of billionaires' influence and responsibility in addressing these issues.

Inspiration and role models: Some billionaires serve as role models and sources of inspiration for aspiring entrepreneurs and individuals seeking success. Their stories of perseverance, innovation, and financial achievements can motivate others to pursue their own dreams and contribute positively to society.

It's important to note that the impact of billionaires on society can be both positive and controversial. While their contributions can bring about positive change, the overall effects depend on the values, actions, and choices made by individual billionaires and how they choose to utilize their wealth and influence.

Chapter 3

The Do's and Don't of a Billionaire:

● __THE DO'S__

As a billionaire, there are several do's that you may consider to maintain your success and make a positive impact. Here are some recommendations:

1. **Invest wisely**: Continually educate yourself about investment opportunities and make informed decisions. Diversify your investments across different asset classes, such as stocks, real estate, bonds, and startups, to minimize risk and maximize returns.

2. **Philanthropy**: Use your wealth to contribute to the betterment of society. Engage in philanthropic activities by supporting causes that align with your values. Establish charitable foundations or

donate to existing organizations to address issues such as poverty, education, healthcare, or environmental conservation.

3. **Continue learning**: Never stop learning and expanding your knowledge. Invest in personal development by attending conferences, seminars, and workshops. Surround yourself with knowledgeable and successful individuals who can inspire and challenge you to grow.

4. **Mentorship**: Share your expertise and experiences with aspiring entrepreneurs and professionals. Offer mentorship programs, internships, or scholarships to support talented individuals who may benefit from your guidance and resources. Help shape the next generation of leaders.

5. **Maintain a strong work ethic**: Remember the principles and work ethic that led to your success. Hard work, dedication, and perseverance are key

factors in achieving and maintaining wealth. Continue to set goals and stay focused on pursuing new opportunities.

6. **Network strategically**: Build and nurture a strong network of professionals, entrepreneurs, and industry leaders. Attend conferences, join industry associations, and participate in events where you can connect with like-minded individuals. Collaborate, share knowledge, and explore potential partnerships.

7. **Prioritize health and well-being**: Your wealth is meaningless without good health. Take care of yourself by maintaining a balanced lifestyle. Engage in regular exercise, eat a nutritious diet, and prioritize mental well-being. Consider supporting healthcare initiatives or organizations that promote wellness.

8. **Long-term thinking**: Develop a long-term perspective on your investments

and endeavors. Avoid short-sighted decisions driven solely by immediate gains. Instead, focus on sustainable growth and projects that have a positive impact on society and the environment.

9. **Continual innovation**: Embrace innovation and stay adaptable to evolving market trends. Foster a culture of creativity and forward-thinking within your businesses. Invest in research and development to stay ahead of the curve and explore new opportunities.

10. **Enjoy life responsibly**: While it's essential to work hard, remember to enjoy the fruits of your labor responsibly. Travel, spend quality time with loved ones, and engage in hobbies and activities that bring you joy. Strive for a work-life balance that allows you to appreciate your success.

• THE DON'T

Here are some "don'ts" for billionaires:

1. **Don't neglect philanthropy:** With great wealth comes great responsibility. Avoid neglecting philanthropic efforts or failing to give back to society. Use your resources to make a positive impact on causes that matter to you and contribute to the well-being of others.

2. **Don't prioritize personal gain over ethics:** Avoid engaging in unethical practices to maximize profits or personal gain. Uphold high moral standards and ensure that your business operations and investments align with ethical principles. Act with integrity and consider the broader implications of your actions.

3. **Don't hoard wealth:** Wealth inequality is a pressing issue in many societies. Avoid excessive accumulation of wealth without actively utilizing it for the greater good.

Consider redistributing or reinvesting your wealth to create opportunities and improve the lives of others.

4. **Don't disregard environmental responsibility:** Climate change and environmental degradation are critical global challenges. Avoid neglecting your environmental responsibilities or contributing to activities that harm the planet. Embrace sustainable practices, invest in clean technologies, and support initiatives that protect and preserve the environment.

5. **Don't ignore social issues:** As a billionaire, you have a platform and influence to address social issues. Don't turn a blind eye to inequality, poverty, or injustice. Use your resources and influence to promote social progress, advocate for marginalized communities, and support initiatives that foster equality and inclusivity.

6. **Don't let wealth isolate you:** Being extremely wealthy can sometimes lead to isolation from the realities of everyday life. Avoid becoming disconnected from the experiences and challenges faced by ordinary people. Stay grounded, engage with diverse perspectives, and actively listen to others' voices.

7. **Don't forget to prioritize personal well-being:** While it's important to be mindful of your responsibilities and obligations, don't neglect your personal well-being. Strive for a balanced life that includes self-care, family time, and personal growth. Remember that wealth alone cannot guarantee happiness and fulfillment.

In the journey to wealth, inspiring billionaires like you may encounter various distractions that can hinder your progress or divert your focus. Here are some common distractions to be mindful of:

1. **Materialistic temptations:** The allure of luxury goods, extravagant lifestyles, and indulgent spending can distract billionaires from their long-term goals. It's important to maintain discipline and avoid excessive materialistic pursuits that may compromise financial stability or dilute the purpose of wealth creation.

2. **Greed and unethical practices:** The pursuit of wealth can sometimes lead to unethical behavior or a desire for more at any cost. It's crucial to stay grounded and uphold ethical values, avoiding shortcuts or engaging in practices that harm others or compromise integrity.

3. **Excessive risk-taking:** While taking risks is often necessary for entrepreneurial success, excessive risk-taking can be

detrimental. It's important to strike a balance between calculated risks and prudent decision-making, ensuring that wealth accumulation is sustainable and not jeopardized by reckless ventures.

4. **Overworking and burnout:** The drive to achieve success can lead to a relentless work ethic, resulting in burnout and neglecting personal well-being. It's essential to prioritize self-care, maintain a healthy work-life balance, and recognize that long-term success requires sustainable efforts.

5. **External pressures and expectations:** Being a billionaire often attracts attention, scrutiny, and expectations from society, friends, and family. It's crucial to stay true to one's vision, values, and goals, without succumbing to external pressures or losing focus due to others' expectations.

6. **Shiny object syndrome:** As opportunities and ventures present themselves, it's easy to get distracted by new and exciting ideas. While exploration is important, it's crucial to maintain focus and evaluate opportunities carefully, ensuring they align with long-term goals and don't lead to unnecessary diversions or resource drain.

7. **Negative influences and distractions:** Surrounding oneself with the wrong people or getting caught up in negative environments can be detrimental. It's important to cultivate a strong support system, associate with like-minded individuals, and avoid distractions that hinder personal growth and progress.

8. **Lack of self-reflection and learning:** Continuous learning, self-reflection, and personal growth are essential for long-term success. Failing to allocate time for self-improvement and acquiring new

knowledge can hinder innovation and personal development.

Chapter 4

The Billionaire's Mindset:

The Billionaire's Mindset is a powerful framework that drives the thinking and actions of those who have achieved extraordinary financial success. It encompasses a set of principles, attitudes, and habits that differentiate billionaires from the average person. Here are some key aspects of the billionaire's mindset:

1. **Visionary Thinking:** Billionaires possess a grand vision that goes beyond the boundaries of what is currently achievable. They think in terms of possibilities and constantly challenge conventional wisdom. They have a clear picture of their desired future and relentlessly pursue their goals.

2. **Growth Mindset:** Billionaires embrace a growth mindset, seeing every challenge as

an opportunity for learning and growth. They understand that setbacks and failures are stepping stones toward success. They are resilient, adaptable, and always open to acquiring new knowledge and skills.

3. **High Ambition:** Billionaires set audacious goals and aim for greatness. They have an unyielding desire to achieve massive success and make a significant impact in their chosen field. They continuously raise the bar and push themselves beyond their comfort zones.

4. **Risk-Taking:** Billionaires are willing to take calculated risks. They understand that great rewards often come with great risks. They carefully assess the potential risks and rewards, and if the odds are in their favor, they take decisive action. They understand that failure is a natural part of the process and use it as a learning opportunity.

5. **Persistence and Determination:** Billionaires are highly resilient and persistent. They do not give up easily and are willing to put in the necessary effort and time to achieve their goals. They understand that success rarely happens overnight and are willing to stay the course, even when faced with obstacles or adversity.

6. **Abundance Mindset:** Billionaires have a mindset of abundance rather than scarcity. They believe that there are abundant opportunities and resources available in the world. They do not view success as a zero-sum game and are willing to collaborate and create win-win situations with others.

7. **Continuous Learning:** Billionaires are voracious learners. They invest heavily in acquiring knowledge, whether through reading books, attending seminars, or surrounding themselves with mentors and

experts. They are constantly seeking new ideas and insights that can propel them forward.

8. **Action-Oriented:** Billionaires have a bias for action. They are not content with simply thinking or planning; they take decisive action to turn their visions into reality. They understand the importance of execution and consistently take steps towards their goals.

9. **Long-Term Thinking:** Billionaires have a long-term perspective. They are not easily swayed by short-term fluctuations or instant gratification. They make strategic decisions that align with their long-term goals, even if it means sacrificing immediate gains.

10.**Philanthropy and Giving Back:** Many billionaires have a strong commitment to giving back to society. They understand the importance of using their wealth and influence to make a positive impact on the world. They actively engage in philanthropy and contribute to causes that align with their values.

It's important to note that while these traits are commonly associated with billionaires, they can also be adopted and cultivated by anyone seeking personal growth and success. The billionaire's mindset is not solely about accumulating wealth; it's about adopting a mindset that empowers you to unlock your full potential and make a difference in your own life and the lives of others.

- **Habits To Develop A Billionaire Mindset:**

Here are some habits to cultivate in order to develop a billionaire mindset:

1. **Think big:** Billionaires have a grand vision for their lives and businesses. They think beyond limitations and focus on expansive possibilities. Train your mind to think on a larger scale and aim for extraordinary achievements.

2. **Set clear goals:** Billionaires are goal-oriented individuals. They set clear, specific, and challenging goals that align with their vision. Break down your goals into actionable steps and regularly **review and adjust them as needed.**

3. **Embrace failure as learning:** Failure is seen as a stepping stone to success for billionaires. Embrace failure as an opportunity to learn, grow, and improve. Develop resilience and perseverance to bounce back from setbacks.

4. **Continuous learning:** Billionaires are lifelong learners. They are constantly seeking knowledge, staying updated with

industry trends, and investing in self-improvement. Read books, attend seminars, take courses, and surround yourself with people who inspire and challenge you.

5. **Take calculated risks:** Billionaires understand that taking risks is essential for growth and success. Assess the risks involved, gather information, and make informed decisions. Be willing to step out of your comfort zone and seize opportunities that have the potential for high returns.

6. **Develop a strong work ethic:** Hard work is a common characteristic among billionaires. Cultivate discipline, dedication, and perseverance in your work. Be willing to put in the time, effort, and energy required to achieve your goals.

7. **Build a strong network:** Billionaires understand the importance of surrounding

themselves with talented and influential individuals. Network strategically and build relationships with like-minded people. Seek mentors who can provide guidance and support your growth.

8. **Stay focused and persistent:** Billionaires maintain laser-like focus on their goals and stay committed to achieving them. Avoid distractions and prioritize tasks that contribute to your long-term success. Maintain persistence in the face of challenges or setbacks.

9. **Develop financial intelligence:** Billionaires possess a deep understanding of finance and investments. Educate yourself on financial matters, learn about different investment vehicles, and develop a solid financial plan. Make informed decisions about money and seek opportunities for wealth creation.

10.Give back and contribute: Many billionaires engage in philanthropy and actively give back to society. Cultivate a mindset of generosity and contribute to causes that align with your values. Making a positive impact on the world can provide a sense of purpose and fulfillment.

Once upon a time, in a small town, lived a young individual named Alex. Born into a modest family, Alex dreamt of a life filled with abundance and success. Determined to achieve their goals, Alex embarked on a journey of self-discovery and wealth creation.

From an early age, when Alex came across some of my posts on social media, he began devouring some of my books on personal development, entrepreneurship, and finance. He understood that knowledge was the key to unlocking their potential. With each page turned, Alex absorbed the wisdom of billionaires, learning their mindset and strategies.

As Alex grew older, he took calculated risks and embraced failures as stepping stones to success. He started their first business, a small online venture, which initially faced challenges. However, Alex persevered, learning from mistakes and constantly improving their strategies. With time, his business gained momentum, and profits began to soar.

Alex surrounded himself with successful individuals, seeking mentors who guided him on his path to greatness. Through networking and building strong relationships, he gained valuable insights and opportunities that propelled his wealth creation endeavors.

But Alex's journey wasn't solely focused on personal gain. He understood the importance of giving back. He established foundations, supported charitable causes, and made a positive impact in their community. By helping others,

Alex found a deeper sense of purpose and fulfillment.

As the years passed, Alex's wealth multiplied exponentially. However, his mindset remained rooted in humility and continuous growth. He never stopped learning, attending conferences and acquiring new skills. Alex diversified his investments, wisely managing his finances and expanding his wealth.

With each success, Alex remained grateful for the journey and the lessons learned. He believed that true wealth extended beyond material possessions, encompassing personal growth, relationships, and making a difference in the world.

As the story of Alex's journey of wealth and success spread, he became an inspiration to many. His billionaire mindset, developed through dedication, resilience, and a thirst for knowledge, served as a testament to the power of dreams and the potential within each individual.

And so, Alex's story became a timeless reminder that anyone, regardless of his background, can cultivate a billionaire mindset and achieve extraordinary success by aligning their thoughts, actions, and ambitions with the principles of abundance, growth, and contribution.

- **Business Ideas That Can Generate Wealth:**

Here are some business ideas that have the potential to generate wealth:

1. **E-commerce Store:** Start an online store selling products in a niche market. You can source products from manufacturers or wholesalers and sell them through your website or established platforms like Amazon or Shopify.

2. **Subscription Box Service:** Create a subscription-based service that delivers curated products or experiences to customers on a recurring basis. This can include anything from beauty products and gourmet foods to books and pet supplies.

3. **Software as a Service (SaaS):** Develop a software application that provides a solution to a specific problem or meets a specific need. Offer it as a subscription-based service, targeting businesses or individuals who can benefit from your software.

4. **Digital Marketing Agency:** Start a digital marketing agency that helps businesses build their online presence, improve search engine rankings, manage social media accounts, and run effective digital advertising campaigns.

5. **Health and Wellness Coaching:** Become a certified health and wellness coach and offer personalized coaching services to individuals or groups. Help clients improve their physical and mental well-being through nutrition, exercise, stress management, and other lifestyle changes.

6. **Renewable Energy Solutions:** Start a business that focuses on renewable energy solutions such as solar panel installation, wind turbine systems, or energy-efficient technologies. This can cater to both residential and commercial clients, helping them reduce their carbon footprint and save on energy costs.

7. **Personalized Learning Platforms:** Develop an online platform that offers personalized learning experiences for students of all ages. Utilize adaptive learning technologies and tailor educational content to individual needs,

providing a more effective and engaging learning environment.

8. **Virtual Reality (VR) Experiences:** Create virtual reality experiences for entertainment, training, or educational purposes. Develop immersive VR games, virtual tours of famous landmarks, or VR simulations for industries like healthcare or aviation.

9. **Sustainable Fashion Brand:** Launch a fashion brand that prioritizes sustainability, using eco-friendly materials, ethical manufacturing practices, and fair trade principles. Cater to conscious consumers who value environmentally friendly and socially responsible products.

10. **Elder Care Services:** Start a business that provides specialized care services for the elderly, such as in-home care, assisted living facilities, or senior transportation

services. With an aging population, there is a growing demand for quality care services.

Remember, the success of any business idea depends on various factors such as market demand, competition, execution, and adaptability. It's important to conduct thorough market research, develop a solid business plan, and continuously innovate to stay ahead in the ever-changing business landscape.

- **List Of Online Investments That Can Generatenerate Wealth:**

Here is a list of online investment options that have the potential to generate wealth:

1. **Stock Market:** Investing in individual stocks or exchange-traded funds (ETFs) can provide substantial returns over time. Platforms like Robinhood,

E*TRADE, and TD Ameritrade offer online trading options.

2. **Mutual Funds:** Mutual funds pool money from multiple investors to invest in a diversified portfolio of stocks, bonds, or other assets. Popular platforms for investing in mutual funds include Vanguard, Fidelity, and Charles Schwab.

3. **Real Estate Crowdfunding:** Online platforms like Fundrise and RealtyMogul allow individuals to invest in real estate projects, offering potential returns through rental income and property appreciation.

4. **Peer-to-Peer Lending:** Platforms such as LendingClub and Prosper enable individuals to lend money directly to others in exchange for interest payments, potentially

earning higher returns compared to traditional savings accounts.

5. **Cryptocurrencies:** Investing in cryptocurrencies like Bitcoin, Ethereum, or other altcoins has gained popularity. Cryptocurrency exchanges like Coinbase and Binance provide platforms for buying and trading digital currencies.

6. **Robo-Advisors:** Robo-advisors such as Betterment and Wealthfront use algorithms to manage investment portfolios based on individual goals and risk tolerance. They offer automated, low-cost investing services.

7. **Online Business:** Starting an online business, such as an e-commerce store or a niche website, can

generate income through sales, advertising, or affiliate marketing.

8. **Dividend Investing:** Investing in dividend-paying stocks can provide a steady income stream. Platforms like Dividend.com and Simply Safe Dividends offer resources and tools for dividend investors.

9. **Forex Trading:** Foreign exchange trading involves buying and selling currencies in the global market. Online brokers like IG and Forex.com provide platforms for forex trading.

10. **Crowdfunding Platforms:** Websites like Kickstarter and Indiegogo allow individuals to invest in early-stage companies or projects, offering the potential for high returns if the venture succeeds.

Remember that investing involves risks, and it's important to do thorough research, understand the risks associated with each investment, and consider your financial goals and risk tolerance before investing any money. It's also advisable to consult with a financial advisor or professional before making any significant investment decisions.

Chapter 5

Conclusion:

In conclusion, the secret to becoming a billionaire is a culmination of various factors and strategies that when combined effectively, can significantly increase your chances of achieving extraordinary wealth. While there is no foolproof formula, certain principles consistently emerge among those who have achieved billionaire status.

First and foremost, a relentless drive and unwavering determination are essential qualities. Becoming a billionaire requires an extraordinary level of ambition, motivation, and a willingness to take risks. Successful billionaires often possess a strong vision and the ability to persevere through setbacks and challenges.

Furthermore, the pursuit of knowledge and continuous learning is crucial. Billionaires tend to be lifelong learners who seek out new information, adapt to changing markets and technologies, and are not afraid to innovate. They invest in their own personal growth, staying updated on industry trends, and surrounding themselves with experts and mentors who can guide them.

In addition, building a strong network and cultivating strategic relationships can play a pivotal role in achieving billionaire status. Collaborations, partnerships, and connections with influential individuals can provide invaluable opportunities, access to resources, and a supportive community. Networking and establishing a reputation for trustworthiness and integrity can open doors and create lucrative partnerships.

Another vital aspect is the ability to identify and seize opportunities. Billionaires have a keen eye for recognizing market gaps, emerging trends, and untapped potentials. They are willing to take calculated risks, make bold moves, and capitalize on favorable circumstances. This requires a combination of analytical skills, a deep understanding of markets, and an intuitive sense of timing.

Finally, the secret to becoming a billionaire lies in creating value for others. Successful billionaires often build their wealth by providing products, services, or solutions that meet a significant demand in the market. By addressing people's needs and improving their lives, billionaires can generate substantial wealth in return.

It is important to note that becoming a billionaire is not solely a measure of success or happiness. It is a personal journey that requires immense dedication, discipline, and sacrifices in various aspects of life. Financial success should be pursued with a broader perspective that encompasses personal growth, ethical responsibility, and the desire to contribute positively to society.

Ultimately, while there is no guaranteed path to becoming a billionaire, embodying qualities such as perseverance, continuous learning, strategic networking, seizing opportunities, and creating value can significantly increase your chances of achieving extraordinary financial success. Remember to pursue your aspirations with integrity, contribute meaningfully, and find fulfillment beyond monetary wealth.

"Unveiling the Wealthy Veil: Inside the Secrets of Billionaires" takes readers on an extraordinary journey into the clandestine world of the ultra-rich, providing a rare glimpse behind the opulent façade that obscures their lives. Throughout the pages of this book, we have uncovered the inner workings of billionaires, delving deep into the untold stories, strategies, and mindset that drive their unprecedented success.

From the outset, it became evident that wealth is not simply a result of luck or circumstance. Instead, it is the culmination of calculated decisions, unwavering determination, and an unwavering commitment to lifelong learning. The secrets of billionaires lie not only in their bank accounts but in their unwavering pursuit of excellence, their insatiable hunger for knowledge, and their ability to adapt and innovate in an ever-changing world.

Through meticulous research and intimate interviews, we have examined the common threads that bind these individuals together. From their unparalleled work ethic and resilience to their ability to identify and seize opportunities, it is clear that the path to extreme wealth is paved with relentless dedication and an unwavering belief in one's own potential.

Yet, "Unveiling the Wealthy Veil" is not merely a guide for aspiring billionaires. It is a testament to the power of human potential, reminding us that success is within reach for those who are willing to push boundaries, challenge conventions, and embrace discomfort. While the billionaire lifestyle may seem unattainable for most, the principles and strategies discussed in this book can be applied to any pursuit, be it personal or professional.

Moreover, this book serves as a cautionary tale, highlighting the potential pitfalls and ethical dilemmas that can accompany extreme wealth. By exploring the stories of billionaires who have navigated the treacherous waters of success, we are reminded of the importance of integrity, compassion, and the responsibility to give back to society.

"Unveiling the Wealthy Veil" invites readers to question their own beliefs about wealth, success, and fulfillment. It challenges us to examine our own ambitions, motivations, and values, urging us to redefine what it truly means to lead a rich and purposeful life.

In closing, this book is a window into a world that few have had the privilege to witness. It is an exploration of the triumphs and tribulations of the world's wealthiest individuals, offering invaluable insights and inspiration for those seeking to unlock their own potential. Through the pages of **"Unveiling the Wealthy Veil: Inside the Secrets of Billionaires**," we have embarked on a transformative journey that will forever alter our perception of wealth and success.